ANIMAL MESSAGES

ANIMAL MESSAGES

SEEK INSPIRATION
FROM YOUR ANIMAL GUIDES

SUSIE GREEN

ILLUSTRATIONS BY
CSABA PASZTOR

CICO BOOKS

London   New York

First published in Great Britain in 2005 by CICO Books

This edition published in the United States in 2007 by CICO Books
an imprint of Ryland, Peters & Small Ltd
341 E 116th St, New York, NY 10029
www.rylandpeters.com

20 19 18 17

Text © Susie Green 2005, 2007
Design and illustration © CICO Books 2005, 2007

CIP data for this title is available from the Library of Congress

ISBN: 978 1 904991 84 7

Printed in China

Designer: David Fordham
Project Editor: Liz Dean
Illustrator: Csaba Pasztor

CONTENTS

Introduction	6
CONNECTING WITH ANIMAL SPIRITS	9
THE CARD GROUPS	12
USING THE CARDS	18
GETTING STARTED	22
SPREADS FOR DIVINATION	24
THE MESSAGES	37
Acknowledgments	64

INTRODUCTION

SINCE THE DAWN OF TIME, man has looked to animals for wisdom, protection, strength, and power. Native Americans and Australian Aborigines identified with animals such as Wolf and Kangaroo, using them as totems to guide and enrich their lives. Chinese and Mongolian shamans were, and still are for many, vital instruments in communicating between the terrestrial and the celestial, the living and their ancestral gods, and they used the power of Tiger and Bear to fly between worlds. South American tribal shamans wore the skin of Jaguar to partake of the animal's extraordinary powers.

When the earth vibrated with animal life and worldwide travel was the sole province of the shaman who could fly not just to the ends of the earth, but to the ends of the universe, people received messages and took power from the creatures they saw around them every day. In India, teaming with monkeys, arose the intelligent, inquisitive, powerful warrior, Shri Hanuman, a zoomorphic Hindu Monkey-god, and the sacred cow, commonplace yet more valuable than gold.

ANIMAL AFFINITY AND URBAN DETACHMENT

GLOBALIZATION, cheap air travel and, above all, television, have made us aware of an extraordinary profusion of animal life. We may feel an affinity to a creature that even one hundred years ago would have been unknowable, or to one who has been part of our natural heritage for all time. Tribal shamans still use the magic of their traditional animals, such as Tiger, even in places such as China where they are extinct, but we are free to receive wisdom and messages from any of the creatures who populate our consciousness or physical reality. And yet paradoxically, urban lifestyles divorce us from the natural world that is our heritage, leaving us less and less in tune with the cosmos. Concrete walls, asphalt roads, and hard pavements separate us even from the earth which conceived us. In our cities the sounds of helicopters, aeroplanes, traffic, and sirens drown out the small sounds of nature that still struggle to be heard.

Such is our lack of harmony with the natural world that many run at the sight of one of the sweetest creatures in the world – tiny, gentle Mouse; while others, terrified, fanatically kill Spider, who does nothing but work tirelessly for man by controlling the ever-spiralling geometric reproduction of insects without the need for pesticides.

In a world where so many of us have infinitely more than we need to live healthily and happily, excessive materialism

RED SQ
GATHER YOUR RESO
SUSTAIN YOU THR

SPIDER
TRAVEL WILL OPEN UP NEW POSSIBILITIES
AND ONE SPECIAL CONNECTION

leads inexorably to the destruction of the forests, meadows, and wetlands that are vital for the myriad marvelous creatures with whom we coexist, and on whose existence we depend for survival. Every time an animal, an insect, a bird, a flower, a plant, or a reptile becomes extinct we lose its magic and wisdom. Every living entity is unique. Nothing can replace the wisdom of the being that is lost and it is we who are the poorer for it.

ANIMAL MESSAGES AND THE WEB OF LIFE

THE PURPOSE OF THESE MESSAGE CARDS is to introduce an understanding of the interconnectedness of everything in life, and a realization of the regeneration that recognition brings. While squashed in the subway, living in air-conditioned isolation in a high-rise, or bowed over a computer it can be so hard to remember that we are an intrinsic part of the web of all life, yet if that web disintegrates we too are lost. For tens of thousands of years we have lived intimately with nature. And, whether we are conscious of it or not, much of the difficulty and stress that particularly urban humankind now experiences is a reflection of its continuing and escalating loss and our increasing alienation from what is our true heritage.

The fifty-two creatures illustrated in the message cards are archetypal in their own way. The stuff of myth, legend, superstition, ritual, and magic for millennia, they all possess rare and remarkable qualities. Spider may fly thousands of feet into the air on her silken threads, while Butterfly can see what we cannot: ultra violet. Elephant appears indomitable, puissant, invincible, but she, like us, can cry and cares tenderly for her calves.

Using the cards is one small way of reconnecting with the greater world around us. Let your animal messengers act as a channel for the energy and sagaciousness of truly magical creatures who are still able to help and heal both us and the earth – if only we are prepared to listen.

Connecting with Animal Spirits

The different energies, skills, wisdom, and magic possessed by every living being ensure that the balance of life on earth is maintained. If top predators such as wolves were to be taken from their ecosystem herbivores would proliferate, leading eventually to overgrazing and the survival of only tough, bitter grasses. As insects and grubs feed off succulent plant-life their population plummets, and in turn insect-eating birds die or must migrate to other ecosystems where they, too, may upset a delicate balance – and so the chain reaction continues. But if the wolf were to come back, harmony would be restored: as herbivores are kept in check, we would see the return of lush vegetation, and with it the insects and their attendant birds.

When an animal unusually crosses your path, visits your dreams, or appears in your cards, it is because it wishes to send you a message specific to its own magical abilities which, if heeded, will restore balance to your life.

Crows, for example, may be a constant in your world, their strong black glossy wings beating the air above, their raucous cries reverberating through the skies – but the day the crow flies close to you and brushes your shoulder with her wing, her presence in your life is changed. The time has come to study her wisdom and magic, to immerse yourself in total harmony with her being, and through this with the living entity that is Gaia, the earth. By opening up to the healing powers of the animal messengers and listening to your intuition, you begin to heal not only yourself but all that surrounds you.

EXPLORING THE SPIRIT OF YOUR ANIMAL

TO ENHANCE YOUR UNDERSTANDING of your messengers and to absorb their wisdom into your life, you may like to spend some time learning how each of them lives and understanding their unique skills. The message cards can only show you certain aspects of their wisdom; in reality, they have many more lessons to impart.

IN THE WILD

NOTHING CAN COMPARE with studying animals in the wild, where their individual energies are palpable forces vibrating in the air. It is impossible to be near Tiger, to see sleek muscles ripple under shining fur, to hear her deep breaths, and not feel her ultimate sensual power; to watch Cheetah silently stalk after long hours of patient waiting and not understand the lessons of predator and prey she teaches; to observe Wolf in the daily life of her pack, and not sense her calm intelligence. A connection is made. The essence of these creatures touches our essence, subtly changing it forever. To know that Peacock's raucous calls are alarm

ORANG-UTAN
WORKING TO LIVE JOYOUSLY, NOT LIVING
TO WORK

signals, telling other jungle denizens of the presence of Tiger, helps you to understand her. To see the jungle react – to hear Monkey take up her cry, to watch Deer melt into the wildwood – teaches you to feel the power of Peacock's protection, and experience the connection which binds all life.

IN THE CITY

OF COURSE, most of us live busy lives in cities and do not have the time to visit the realms of Wolf, of Kangaroo, and Whale. But nature surrounds us even so. Crow lives in large cities from São Paulo to London, Squirrel leads her busy life in parks and suburbs throughout the world, Fox has ventured into many urban spaces, Spider lurks in attic and garden, and Frog makes her home in the tiniest of garden ponds. Taking the time to watch the daily drama of their lives as they resourcefully integrate into our territory, skillfully find sources of food, and raise and school their young, will connect you ever more deeply with the web of life and the wisdom it contains.

FROG
ADAPT AND SURVIVE BY ACCEPTING THE
INEVITABLE AND SEIZING POTENTIAL

OTHER WAYS TO CONNECT

EAGLE
CREATE YOUR VISION

ALTHOUGH ZOOS SERVE a genuinely useful purpose in conserving animals whose existence is endangered, it is not recommended that you observe your messengers there. Their spirits are depleted, their natural way of living taken. There is nothing to be learned from a Crocodile who cannot snatch an unwary deer from the river bank, from an Eagle who cannot soar or an Elephant who cannot live her complex and social family life. However, watching natural history programs and reading the works of naturalists and zoologists will reap great dividends. The minute observation required in drawing or painting your animal messengers will also bring their spirits closer to you so they can communicate with you in ways that will truly revolutionize your life.

THE CARD GROUPS

ALTHOUGH EACH MESSENGER has her own unique qualities and particular lessons to impart, she also has wisdom in common with the other messengers who, for instance, live in the waters or make the trees their home. For this reason the animal cards are divided into six groups, which reflect underlying similarities: creatures of the air, arboreal creatures, earth-dwellers, walkers between worlds, water denizens, and land creatures. If a preponderance of messengers from any one group appears when you consult the cards, then that set's wisdom will have an underlying meaning for you.

CREATURES OF THE AIR:

EAGLE, RAVEN, OWL, HUMMING BIRD, PARROT, PEACOCK, BUTTERFLY, BAT, SPIDER, AND BEE

EAGLE
CREATE YOUR VISION

BY DIFFERENT MEANS all these creatures escape the confines of earth. They soar above material cares and worries and counsel that it is time to let go of our cares, to leave the past firmly behind you where it belongs, and to look for a new future where anything is possible. Spider uniquely makes her gossamer home in the air, connected to earth by silken ties almost too fine to perceive. She counsels that as you go forward in life you should remain attached to your past, but not be dominated by it.

PEACOCK
PROTECT YOUR HEART FROM THOSE WHO MAY
CHEAT BEFORE THEY HURT YOU

BLACK PANTHER
SENSUALITY AND PASSION STIR BENEATH A
CLOAK OF SECRECY

ARBOREAL CREATURES:

PANTHER, PANDA, SLOTH, ORANG-UTAN, CHAMELEON, AND RED SQUIRREL

RED SQUIRREL
GATHER YOUR RESOURCES NOW, FOR THEY WILL
SUSTAIN YOU THROUGH COMING CHANGE

THESE ANIMALS MAKE THEIR HOMES in warm, protective trees. With green, rustling foliage, these vital lungs of our world breathe out oxygen, inducing in arboreal messengers relaxation and sleep. They counsel that your home should be your sanctuary, an oasis of calm, repose, and tranquility, from which you may venture refreshed.

Your home environment profoundly affects your wellbeing. If it is a stressful place, finally it becomes a

CHAMELEON
CONCEAL AMBITION WITH PATIENCE UNTIL IT IS
TIME TO MAKE YOUR MOVE

prison from which you wish only to escape. Arboreal creatures advise that if your home life is unhappy, due to friction in personal relationships, because you bring your work home with you, or because your surroundings are made uncongenial by noise or disagreeable neighbors, it is time for change, no matter how radical.

EARTH-DWELLERS:

MOUSE, PORCUPINE, BADGER, SCORPION, AND FOX

MOUSE
BE PERSISTENT AND INCISIVE AND ALL OBSTACLES
WILL BE OVERCOME

THESE MESSENGERS MAKE THEIR HOMES within the safe, secure, and embracing element of the earth itself, and counsel that you too should remain grounded. If material anxieties and worries are dominating your mind, they advise that you pay attention to what is truly important in life – your family, your true friends, your partner, and nature.

Earth-dwellers counsel that you reconnect with the wild world, even if this is as ephemeral as walking in a city park.

FOX
YOUR SHARPENED SENSES ALLOW YOU TO OBSERVE
THE ACTIONS OF OTHERS

BADGER
ABANDON COMPROMISE AND FIGHT VALIANTLY
FOR WHAT YOU BELIEVE IN

The grass may be manicured, the earth trodden hard, but beneath the surface worms and insects work tirelessly to renew the soil and its touch beneath bare feet can stabilize you, even when much seems lost.

WALKERS BETWEEN WORLDS:

TIGER, HIPPOPOTAMUS, WATER BUFFALO, BEAVER, AND ELEPHANT

TIGER
PASSION AND ADVENTURE BECKON

WE DO NOT ALWAYS THINK of these messengers in connection with water, but it is vital to their well-being and intrinsic to their natures. Swimming powerfully from island to island, Tiger colonized Bali and Java and strove for Hong Kong; today, she swims in the vast rivers of the Sunderban's mangrove swamps, perfectly adapted to drink its salty waters. Hippopotamus cruises in the waters of Africa, and Buffalo in the rivers of Asia; Elephant moves gracefully through the waters of the Bay of Bengal, and bathes daily for her health.

BEAVER
INVESTING IN HOME COMFORTS PROVIDES
SECURITY AND FAMILY TOGETHERNESS

Walkers between worlds counsel that you too should inhabit two planes. Neglecting the spiritual in favor of the material will cause our inner essential selves to suffer, but because we are of the material world we must also attend to its demands. These messengers also advise us that the needs of both work and home must be finely balanced for fulfillment and happiness.

WATER DENIZENS:

WHALE, DOLPHIN, CRAB, RAY, SEAL, OCTOPUS, CROCODILE, AND FROG

SEAL
HARD WORK AND INSPIRATION ARE THE
FOUNDATION OF THEIR CREATIVITY

THESE CREATURES MAKE the waters their primary home, drawing strength from this primeval element and flourishing thanks to its bounty.

The greatest of these, Whale, lives on plankton, the tiniest of organisms, while the most ancient, Crocodile,

OCTOPUS
TRAVEL ACROSS EARTH AND OVER SEA TO
SECURELY EMBRACE YOUR DREAM

seeks flesh and blood. They counsel that you too may be nourished in myriad ways – that the seemingly insignificant can be the seed of the mightiest creation, as can the most obvious and celebrated.

LAND CREATURES:

CHEETAH, LION, COBRA, KANGAROO, HARE, WOLF, RHINO, MOUNTAIN GOAT, LLAMA, WILD BOAR, WILD HORSE, SCARAB BEETLE, BEAR, DEER, BISON, MOOSE, BABOON, AND TORTOISE

HARE
DISCERNMENT BEFORE A PASSIONATE ENCOUNTER
LEADS TO THE MAGIC OF LOVE

A GREAT NUMBER OF our messengers live on the earth's varied terrain and have adapted in very specific ways to the other animals, birds, flowers, rocks, insects, and climate they are confronted with.

Cheetah has taken the form of a sight hound to sprint at 70 miles – over 110 kilometers – per hour, Tortoise makes

BEAR
NURTURING CREATIVITY AND RETURN TO THE
SWEETNESS OF LIFE

BABOON
IN LOVE AND DECLARATIONS OF PASSION
HEARTFELT COMMUNICATION IS THE KEY

her carapace her fortress, Baboon's sexual desires are broadcast through vivid-colored fleshy swellings of purple and red. None is better than another, for all are perfect in their world. The lesson these animal messengers teach is that there are myriad ways to live and infinite paths to choose, all with their own validity.

We are not all geniuses – we cannot all be film stars, city millionaires, or even Buddhist monks – but we all can choose paths and lifestyles to suit our own intrinsic nature. Some thrive on the thrills of cutting a deal, others find deep satisfaction in devoting themselves to their families. Still others crave to travel the world. No way is right, no way wrong, and finally only we can choose. What is important is that like our animal messengers we are not swayed by the judgments of others nor by slick advertising, which seeks to make us hold the empty belief that objects that we never knew we needed will make us happy. Scarab Beetle dines on the waste of others, an anathema to a world which constantly discards old to buy new. But Scarab is a flawless, living jewel.

SCORPIO
IN A NEW RELATIONSHIP
CHALLENGE OF EGO

WILD BOAR
WHATEVER TRADITION OR OTHERS EXPECT OF
YOU, ONLY TO YOURSELF BE TRUE

RAVEN
INTUITION TO RECEIVE A
THE WORLD OF SPIRIT

USING THE CARDS

WHEN FIRST YOU TOUCH your deck of animal message cards, you establish a vital connection that deepens as the cards absorb your energy, the blueprint of your life force.

There are many ways to enhance this process of connection with your messengers. One of the most simple is to wrap the cards in a scarf of natural material, silk, cotton or wool, dyed in hues sympathetic to the environments of your messengers – the deep blue-greens of the boundless oceans or the rich red-browns of fertile earth – and place them under your pillow. While you dream, you infuse the cards with your essence and engage with your messengers as you sleep. Another is to look at your cards and meditate on the nature of each animal, allowing their energies to enter your spirit, which enhances the confluence and increases the clarity of the messages your animal guides send to you.

CREATING AN ATMOSPHERE FOR A READING

ONCE YOU FEEL THAT THE TIME has come to consult them, it is beneficial to create an atmosphere sympathetic to your messengers. This welcomes their spirits into your presence and demonstrates to them your sincerity and the belief in their powers, which is necessary for a true, revealing, and relevant reading. You can use the message cards at home, finding a soothing space which you can sanctify with soft light and perfume, or surround yourself in nature by simply sitting in a garden or even a city park at a peaceful time of day.

SCENT

HEADY INCENSE SUCH AS frankincense and galbanum has been used as an aid to meditation and a means of connecting to other worlds for thousands of years. Their exquisite, intoxicating fragrances create a magical aura that is inviting to your messengers and inspiring for your soul. Of course, the earth is abundant in wild perfumes: rose, jasmine, neroli, vetiver, and hyacinth, for example, all vibrate and resonate in their own specific way. Any that appeal to you are suitable, as is the delicious perfume of freshly cut flowers.

LIGHT

THE HARSH GLARE of neon or white light is inimical to animals; walk at night with a torch, and every animal flees from its artificial glare. Natural sunlight, the clear beam of the full moon, or the soft, gentle light of beeswax candles are all conducive to your messengers' presence. The ritual of lighting a candle signifies moving into another world. The candle's subtle fragrance will blend with that of your chosen perfume medium and the soothing flicker of the flame will help your mind relax and open.

REDRESSING YOUR BALANCE

YOUR ANIMAL MESSENGERS wish to heal and guide you, but for their magic to work you need to be open to their wisdom and approach them with respect and humility. Often, even the most complex or emotional of problems have their root in some kind of imbalance in the way we live our lives. But sometimes this can be difficult to accept, so unconsciously we construct a tissue of deception and illusion for ourselves which prevents our progress on life's path.

If suffering from truly painful unrequited love, for instance, we may try to fill an emotional void in our lives without taking on the demands of a real relationship, or neglect other areas of our lives which could be fulfilling. Romantic love is a part of life, but it is not its entirety. The workaholic may be fearful of intimacy, and so uses the demands of work as a reason to avoid it. The put-upon employee who always works overtime for free and takes lunch at his desk needs to leave fear behind and cultivate assertiveness and the ability to say no.

We may be constantly tired, pressured, anxious, jealous, fearful, tearful, or even full of hate, but if we trust to our messengers, consult them with sincerity, and then heed their advice, we may redress the imbalance the animals perceive in our lives. In this way our lives will become transformed, redolent with meaning and joy. And, by allowing the animal spirits to heal us we not only restore our own balance but make a tiny step towards redressing the balance of the distressed earth on which we live.

With the exception of Cheetah, who can foretell the need for a fast decision with possibly life-changing consequences, the wisdom of the other messengers takes a little time to work. We cannot change our lives all at once; we are too human and the patterns of our lives too powerful, but if every day we make a genuine effort to live our lives differently – to see its whole through the wisdom of the animals – sooner than we might imagine we can become the people we always knew we could be.

MOUSE
BE PERSISTENT AND INCISIVE AND ALL OBSTACLES
WILL BE OVERCOME

RED SQUIRREL
GATHER YOUR RESOURCES NOW, FOR THEY WILL
SUSTAIN YOU THROUGH COMING CHANGE

OWL
SEEK OUT DEEPER KNOWLEDGE TO SEE
THROUGH DECEPTION

GETTING STARTED

SIT COMFORTABLY where you will not be disturbed, in your peaceful space at home or in nature (see page 19). Unwrap your cards and lay the cloth out before you. As mentioned earlier (see page 18) it is best to keep them wrapped in cloth made from natural fiber, such as silk or cotton, whose color you find soothing and inspiring.

USING THE MESSAGE CARDS DAILY TO FIND LIFE BALANCE

YOU CAN CALL UPON YOUR ANIMAL MESSENGERS for guidance in finding balance in your life. All you need do is choose one card, every day or each week. Begin by shuffling the cards slowly, and have them facing toward you, so you can see and touch every card. When you have done so, keep shuffling, but now close your eyes. Meditate on each animal's qualities and imagine them in their natural environments, using their unique magical skills and wisdom. When their images fill your mind it is time to ask your animal messengers for their help and guidance. Ask them to connect with you, either aloud or silently.

Lay out the cards face down, in the shape of a fan. Let your hand drift slowly over the cards and pick the one you are most drawn to. This will be your true messenger for the day ahead.

INTERPRETING YOUR MESSAGES

WHEN YOU READ THE KEY to your messenger's meaning (see pages 38–63) a way forward should present itself. Sometimes the solution may be very simple. If you are tired and always running around, the presence of Red Squirrel, who dashes and scurries through her woods, is a message for you to slow down. Your messenger is confirming what in your heart you know to be the case. We all make excuses for why we must be busy, but for whom are we doing this? Our work suffers because we are never refreshed, our families and friends suffer because they never see us, and in the end we may even become ill.

Alternatively, perhaps you are bored, with little to tempt and excite you. From lack of stimulation you retire early, but because you are not tired your sleep is fitful. The next day you feel even less inclined to actively join the world, compounding your ennui. In this case, Red Squirrel counsels you to become busy like her. As she finds nuts in times of plenty and buries them in the earth for times of hardship, so should you begin to construct your future in the outside world. Trust in your messenger and restore the inner energy to your life. You will accomplish far more than you would ever have imagined.

Should you feel at all unclear about the message an animal spirit is sending to you, spend a few moments imagining the animal in its natural environment and consider how your situation relates to this. Your messenger's advice will soon become clear.

SPREADS FOR DIVINATION

YOU CAN LAY OUT the message cards in particular formations, or spreads, to divine answers in a structured way. This is helpful when you have a particular problem that you want to look at in greater detail, or perhaps you have to make an important decision, or find a new path in life. Because the seeds of your future are unfolding from your past, your animal messengers can see the way forward for you. Consult their wisdom by using the following relevant spreads.

PEACOCK
PROTECT YOUR HEART FROM THOSE WHO MAY
CHEAT BEFORE THEY HURT YOU

THE THREE-CARD SPREAD

USED FOR HUNDREDS OF YEARS, the Three-card Spread shows the past, present, and future. Capable of giving an overview of life or concentrating on a detail, its very simplicity means the animal messages come through with extraordinary clarity.

Shuffle the cards while concentrating on your question. When you feel that the animal spirits have heard your question, open your eyes and with your left hand cut the deck twice, laying down three piles of cards face down. Now replace the piles in a different order and deal the first three cards from the top of the deck, face down. Place them left to right as shown. Turn them over in order and the story behind your question will be revealed.

1 The past
2 The present
3 The future

       1   2   3

EXAMPLE

IF YOU WERE TO ASK YOUR MESSENGERS about prosperity, and you drew Beaver, Lion, and Cheetah, this would reveal that in the past you have been like Beaver: resourceful, creative, and protective of your assets. Languorous Lion, in the present position, shows a need to keep your work/life equilibrium, as exhausting yourself for material gain will only detract from precious relationships with friends and family. In the future is Cheetah, who shows the path forward. She speeds up events, brings opportunities that must be grasped and, as a symbol of duality, reveals the possibility of a business partner with whom to share your ambition and workload. Overall, the reading predicts success borne of an astute attitude and hard work.

THE FUTURE UNFURLED

THIS SPREAD IS BASED ON an ancient Druidic system of divination which has helped infinite numbers of people chart a path through life. You can use it when you need to come to a decision – whether to abandon or go forward with projects or relationships, for example – or to assess where your life is just now and what you can expect if you continue on this path.

1 **The foundation of the matter**
2 **The immediate past**
3 **The situation at present**
4 **How you are adding positively to the situation**
5 **External influences working in your favor**
6 **Your own negative input**
7 **External influences working against you**
8 **The immediate future**
9 **The ultimate future**

SHUFFLE THE CARDS while mulling over your specific question or general query as to what path your life is taking. When you feel that the messengers have heard you, lay the cards face down in the order shown in the illustration.

Turn them over one at a time and take in the meaning and energies of each card before moving to the next. Only when you have fully absorbed all the animal messengers' wisdom in each position will you be able to look at the spread and understand the entirety of its meaning. When you have absorbed the wisdom the cards impart, you should be able to see another way forward.

To clarify if a particular or action or change of energy rights the situation, shuffle the remaining messenger cards and spread them in a fan face down. When you feel drawn to one card in particular pull it from the pack and place it next to card number 9. The message will reveal with clarity if your meditations and conclusions have been correct.

CARD 1 shows the foundation of the future. It explains the energies from the past, good and/or bad, which have lead inevitably to your current position.

CARD 2 reveals the immediate past. At first sight, this seems redundant. After all, you have just lived your immediate past, so why should you need a messenger to explain it? Often, however, we perceive things wrongly. For example, if an important letter fails to arrive we blame the sender and fail to contact them in return, setting up a whole chain of unfortunate events. It may be, however, that the letter was lost in the post or wrongly delivered, and the sender is hurt or angry at your failure to reply. This card will reveal the true past, rather than your perception of it. This knowledge alone can transform your future.

CARD 3 shows how the situation rests at present or, if you are seeking wisdom on your life's path, where you stand at this time. Is it a place you want to be? Meditate carefully on this crucial point and consider the wisdom in cards 4, 5, 6, and 7 in relation to it.

CARD 4 reveals your own energies and actions that are having a positive effect on the situation and/or leading to a fruitful future on your life's path. These wisdoms are to be cultivated.

CARD 5 reveals external benign influences. This includes the energies and actions of those around you as well as the greater state of the world.

CARD 6 reveals your own energies and actions that are working against a particular outcome you desire or are hindering your progress on life's path. Even if the ultimate outcome as shown in card number 9 is positive, it is always advisable to meditate upon your messenger's wisdom and consider how this negative influence can be further mitigated.

CARD 7 reveals the actions and energies of others that are preventing the outcome you wish, or conditions in the wider world that mitigate against your progress.

CARD 8 reveals the immediate future, that which will come to be in the next few days or weeks. This card may be positive or negative. Neither is important, for situations are constantly turning. Victory may be snatched from the jaws of defeat just as injudicious action might ruin a plan, project, or relationship that seemed certain to succeed.

CARD 9 shows the ultimate results of your deeds, desires, and energies. If this card is positive and in accord with your wishes, the wisdom of the animals is already with you and it is judicious to continue without deviation upon your path. If this card shows an undesirable result you must consider all the cards in the spread carefully, but particularly numbers 2, 3, 6, and 7.

THE PATH OF THE HEART

THE HEART SPREAD IS DESIGNED to help you not only understand the emotions of your own heart but that of the other person. It is equally suitable to clarify feelings in a nascent relationship yet to evolve due to the reluctance of either party to make those all-important first moves, or one of several years' standing where ties have become uncertain.

Passion and romance are an intrinsic part of being human. To love and wish to be loved in return is fundamental to our way of being. Because so much of our happiness is at stake, when we venture to make our passion known or to deepen a light-hearted romance to something more serious and lasting, we often are nervous or shy, over excitable, or tongue-tied. Sometimes when another has attempted to make their feelings known to us we do not respond as we might wish, nervous of making fools of ourselves, wondering in our hearts if they really meant what we thought they did, or if longing and desire made us hear only what we wanted. Celebrity, power, wealth, achievement, and even overwhelming sexual attractiveness count for nothing when the heart is involved.

Shuffle your animal message cards thoroughly, thinking deeply on the situation between you and the other person and keep their image firmly in your mind. When you feel that the messengers have heard your question, lay out the cards face down in the order shown in the illustration overleaf. Then turn them over one by one.

1 Current love dynamic
2 The effect of your feelings and lifestyle on the relationship
3 Innermost, hidden hopes and fears for the relationship

4 How you respond to the other person on an intellectual level
5 The immediate future
6 The effect of the other person's feelings and lifestyle on the relationship

7 The other person's innermost hidden hopes and fears for the relationship
8 How the other person responds to you on an intellectual level

9 How the other person will behave toward you in the immediate future
10 How your relationship will ultimately develop

CARD 1, the base of the heart, shows the current dynamics between the two of you. Deer in this position, for instance, might indicate modesty or nervousness; Cobra, profound feelings waiting for expression.

CARDS 2, 3, 4, AND 5, climbing the left wall of the heart, reveal your part in the matter.

CARD 2 shows how your general feelings and lifestyle are currently affecting the matter. Red Squirrel here, for example, might mean that you have been too busy to give the relationship the time it deserves.

CARD 3 shows your innermost hopes and fears for the relationship, something you may not even have admitted to your conscious self. Sometimes when what we *think* we want becomes reality, we discover that our innermost self wanted something completely different.

CARD 4 reveals how you see the person on an intellectual level.

CARD 5 shows the immediate future.

CARDS 6, 7, 8, AND 9, climbing the right hand wall of the heart, show the other person's part in the matter.

CARD 6 shows how the other person's general feelings and lifestyle currently affect the situation.

CARD 7 shows their innermost hopes and fears for the relationship, which may or may not mirror their outwardly perceived behavior.

CARD 8 reveals how the other person sees you on an intellectual level.

CARD 9 shows their behavior towards you in the immediate future. For instance, Goat in this position could indicate that the other person will fight fiercely for your love.

CARD 10 reveals how any longer term relationship will develop between the two of you.

THE ANIMALS OF THE FOUR CORNERS

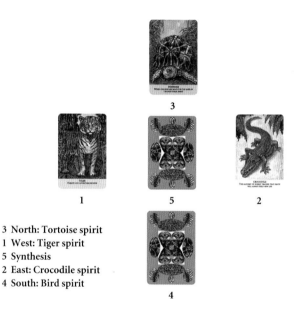

3

1   **5**   **2**

3 North: Tortoise spirit
1 West: Tiger spirit
5 Synthesis
2 East: Crocodile spirit
4 South: Bird spirit

4

THE CHINESE ANCIENTS divided the heavens and its multiple microcosmic reflections on the earth's surface into four quarters: Vermillion Bird ruled the south, Black Tortoise the north, Azure Dragon, embodiment of masculine energy or yang, the east, and White Tiger, symbol of feminine power or yin, the west.

The Chinese saw the reflections of these mighty creatures' bodies in the very earth around them, and they believed that the places where the sexual energies of these creatures crossed contained the very essences of life-giving energy – and were therefore the most propitious of places to live. Taoist practitioners of sexual yoga also acknowledge this powerful confluence, calling their art the yoga of the White Tiger and the Azure Dragon.

For these reasons, The Animals of the Four Corners spread is helpful in divining both if a change of residence or country are favorable, and if romance will prosper.

Take Tortoise, Tiger, and Crocodile, Dragon's earthly ambassador, from the pack and place them in their allotted positions. Shuffle the remaining cards carefully thinking deeply on the person who interests you or the place you wish to move to. When you are satisfied, place one card to the south [4] and one to the center [5].

CARD 4 Should a bird messenger occupy the south, a very favorable outcome is expected: Parrot, Eagle, Raven, Peacock, Owl, or Humming Bird. A non-bird messenger in the south means the result is variable, so meditate deeply on the qualities of its messenger to find the correct way forward.
CARD 5 indicates the final result, the effect upon your well-being and energy if you proceed as planned.

It should, however, be remembered that in some circumstances the messenger may be completely contrary to your desires. For instance, if you had enquired would a lover be true and Goat were to appear in position 4 or position 5, the likelihood would be that you are but one of many, for Goat maintains a harem – although this would not preclude him fighting passionately for your affections.

THE SCARAB

SCARAB SYMBOLIZES the triumph of life over death, of creativity over stagnation. She takes the discarded and unregarded and transforms it. For Scarab, everything has potential for growth. This means that her spread is useful in determining how projects will progress. This encompasses the development of artistic creations, business enterprises big and small, and can even indicate if studying for a particular career or qualification will bear fruit.

4

3

2

4 **Fruition**
3 **Metamorphosis**
2 **Preparation**
1 **Germination**

CARD 1 Germination: the egg lies in wait

All the elements of fruition are nascent within the seed. Your animal messenger shows the potential for your project and its overriding energy. Is this in accord with your vision?

CARD 2 Preparation: Scarab as larva takes the steps necessary to prepare for metamorphosis

Scarab's larvae feed on the nutrients that surround it. Are you giving your project the attention, energy, and dedicated work it needs in order to grow?

1

CARD 3 Metamorphosis: Scarab undergoes transformation in her mummy-like pupa

This is the moment at which your project struggles to take form. When the research for a book must be turned into prose, or the carefully selected stock brought together in a shop. Are you content with the shape your project now has or must further work be done?

CARD 4 Fruition: Scarab bursts forth from her underground chamber

This shows how your project will manifest in the material world – if the rewards you expect, be they inner fulfillment, satisfaction at a job well done, wealth, or peer acclaim, are to be yours.

THE MESSAGES

CONSTANT IN THEIR WISDOM, your animal messengers wait patiently, as they have always done, for you to discover them. Since before the dawn of history they have inspired, warned, and guided humankind whenever they called for assistance with respect and honor, and continue to do so today.

Draw strength from their images, knowing that their loving spirits are yours to conjure into everyday reality whenever you are confused, downhearted, or unsure of what path to take. All you have to do is ask.

BAT
YOU HAVE THE POWER TO TR/
AND MOVE INTO A LIMITL

WATER BUFFALO
FACE LIFE HEAD-ON WITH COURAGE AND RECLAIM
THE BRAVE SPIRIT WITHIN YOU

PORCUPINE
FEND YOURSELF HONORABLY
JYING YOURSELF HONORABLY
OTING THOSE CLOSE TO YOU

EAGLE
CREATE YOUR VISION

EAGLE

CREATE YOUR VISION

Magical, majestic **EAGLE** soars and swoops through the air before diving to grasp the fruits of the earth. Her vision senses a rabbit moving a mile in the distance, but to you she gives vision that unveils the past, encompasses the present, and reveals the future. Events will move swiftly from now on, so use the power of Eagle wisely to develop your spirituality and consciously create your dream or your vision of the future. Consider too the power of karma, which is implicit in your every action or inaction.

RAVEN

LISTEN TO YOUR INTUITION TO RECEIVE A MESSAGE FROM THE WORLD OF SPIRIT

RAVEN
LISTEN TO YOUR INTUITION TO RECEIVE A
MESSAGE FROM THE WORLD OF SPIRIT

Black, glossy magician of the feathered world, intelligent denizen of windswept hills, lonely crags, and dark forest, **RAVEN** swoops on wings of four-foot span. He calls to the wolves to tell them that a feast awaits, a deer, a bear; and he calls to you so that you may discover the enchanter within, and give form to the formless. Listen carefully to his cry, for Raven brings you a message from the realm of the spirit.

OWL

<small>SEEK OUT DEEPER KNOWLEDGE
TO SEE THROUGH
DECEPTION</small>

OWL
SEEK OUT DEEPER KNOWLEDGE TO SEE
THROUGH DECEPTION

If **OWL** has glided into your cards, the time has come to seek the hidden as Owl seeks prey beneath the deep, crisp snow. Arcane knowledge, deep within the ageless traditions of white magic, will now reveal itself if you quiet your mind and explore the mysteries beyond; your perceptions will be such that others will be utterly unable to deceive you. Like Owl you will absorb the benign and nourishing and discard the destructive, imbuing your life with intense meaning.

HUMMING BIRD
TURN AWAY FROM INFIDELITY SO THAT
LOVE MAY BLOSSOM

HUMMING BIRD

<small>TURN AWAY FROM INFIDELITY
SO THAT LOVE MAY BLOSSOM</small>

Delicate beauty of balmy, sun-kissed climes, **HUMMING BIRD** is faithful to the blossoms that nourish her and knows that there is little more injurious to love than infidelity. If a partner is unfaithful

it is time to soar away and taste the affection of another. If you no longer love exclusively, fly away before you bruise their being and take away something essential from your own soul that will leave you less open to love the next time it is offered.

PARROT

LET SUNSHINE REVITALIZE YOUR
SOUL AND COLOR TRANSFORM
YOUR WORLD

PARROT, wondrous and vivid, her plumage that
of the rainbow, her demeanor that of the
animating sun, has flown to your cards to
remind you that your surroundings truly are
your life. The color of a room influences mood,
balmy cloudless lands stimulate energy and
revitalize the soul. If your heart has been telling
you to move to another home, even another
continent, but your mind has been finding reasons not to, Parrot counsels
that the time has come to listen to your intuitive desire.

PARROT
LET SUNSHINE REVITALIZE YOUR SOUL AND COLOR
TRANSFORM YOUR WORLD

PEACOCK

PROTECT YOUR HEART FROM
THOSE WHO MAY CHEAT BEFORE
THEY HURT YOU

PEACOCK's call warns of the dangerous
approach of Tiger and Cobra. As forest denizens
heed and flee, so you should now fly from the
concrete jungle's double dealer and heart-
breaker. Cosmic vehicle of Kama, Hindu god of
love, Peacock knows that although the first
declarations of love may be attended by flowers
or offerings of ambrosial foods, true intimacy

PEACOCK
PROTECT YOUR HEART FROM THOSE WHO MAY
CHEAT BEFORE THEY HURT YOU

develops later, in seclusion and simplicity. Outward show is a ritual and
should not be confused with the realities of long-lasting relationships.

BUTTERFLY

DELIGHT IN LIFE AND EMBRACE
CHANGE AS THE SOURCE OF
YOUR CREATIVITY

BUTTERFLY
DELIGHT IN LIFE AND EMBRACE CHANGE AS THE
SOURCE OF YOUR CREATIVITY

As iridescent wings unfurl from a hard chrysalis, change incarnate, the **BUTTERFLY** is born. Some cross raging oceans, their apparent fragility belying their strength and endurance, some sip the flower's sweet nectar for only a day, but all dance. The butterfly arrives to remind you to delight in life, to take time to experience what you love and to embrace the changes she brings as the source of your own creativity. Through kindness and tenderness you will attain your goals.

BAT

YOU HAVE THE POWER TO
TRANSCEND FAILURE AND MOVE
INTO A LIMITLESS FUTURE

BAT
YOU HAVE THE POWER TO TRANSCEND FAILURE
AND MOVE INTO A LIMITLESS FUTURE

BAT once crawled upon the earth, but she reached for the stars and now she really can fly. If you have pulled Bat to guide you, you too can become anything you want. But remember, everything has its own period of gestation and as you progress to your own limitless future you must transcend failure and its attendant fear, that of striving again. With failure comes the knowledge that brings you ever nearer your heart's goal until on the destined day you are reborn.

SPIDER

TRAVEL WILL OPEN UP NEW POSSIBILITIES AND ONE SPECIAL CONNECTION

SPIDER
TRAVEL WILL OPEN UP NEW POSSIBILITIES
AND ONE SPECIAL CONNECTION

SPIDER flies on silken strands through azure skies and brooding storms, and knows that the time has come to expand your horizons. Travel, be it to faraway lands or a flower-strewn meadow, and see the world through new eyes, with the deep understanding that nothing is impossible. Spider sees her world through touch, not light, translating vibration into knowledge. Take wisdom from what you cannot see and if the fleeting touch of another affects you, acknowledge that connection and allow it to flourish.

BEE

HARD WORK IS REWARDED WITH RESPONSIBILITY AND A SWEETNESS THAT IS SHARED

BEE
HARD WORK IS REWARDED WITH RESPONSIBILITY
AND A SWEETNESS THAT IS SHARED

Without busy **BEE** pollinating the flowers whose rich produce of fruit, vegetable, and seed provides for man, beast, and bird, the world's ecosystems would decay and the web of life unravel. If Bee has come to you now, she is asking you to look within: do you wisely protect or thoughtlessly pollute her environment? One of the most powerful creatures on earth, Bee works hard, but just as her honey makes warm intoxicating mead, she reminds us, too, that a life without frolic and fun lacks sweetness.

BLACK PANTHER

SENSUALITY AND PASSION
STIR BENEATH A CLOAK OF
SECRECY

Black and silky as the velvet night, puissant icon of feminine sensuality and sexual energies yet holding within the power of the male, lithe **BLACK PANTHER** counsels that the time has come to awaken passion, to accept and reclaim your intrinsic sexuality and in so doing, embrace life. Panther is stealth incarnate, her quarry has no intimation of her coming. Like Panther hide your intentions until the time for action has come, or risk losing advantage, be it in love or business.

BLACK PANTHER
SENSUALITY AND PASSION STIR BENEATH A
CLOAK OF SECRECY

PANDA

ENJOY THE SANCTUARY OF
SOLITUDE TO REGAIN SELF-
ESTEEM AND TRANQUILITY

PANDA
ENJOY THE SANCTUARY OF SOLITUDE TO REGAIN
SELF-ESTEEM AND TRANQUILITY

Self-contained and content in her serried banks of bamboo, tranquil **PANDA** relaxes in her world of plenty and ease, dependent upon none. Sometimes we become too wrapped up in others, dependent upon their approval, and wither inside should they withhold it. Wise Panda counsels that time spent in a peaceful, established sanctuary, retreating far away from your daily life both physically and mentally, will fortify your spirit and allow your true self, not someone else's image of you, to flourish.

SLOTH
CONSIDER THE SMALLNESS OF YOUR NEEDS AND
TREASURE WHAT YOU POSSESS

SLOTH

CONSIDER THE SMALLNESS OF YOUR NEEDS AND TREASURE WHAT YOU POSSESS

Humankind gave **SLOTH** this name, seeing in the apparent stillness of her neo-tropical rainforest life mere laziness, but Sloth is virtue incarnate: a perfectly balanced ecosystem. Impregnable to predators, surrounded by nourishment and bathed by the sun, Sloth is proof to those much stronger and more active that she wants for nothing and wastes nothing. She counsels that you treasure that which surrounds you. Squander neither love nor material things, even if they are no longer new. Then, like Sloth, relax in true prosperity.

ORANG-UTAN

WORKING TO LIVE JOYOUSLY, NOT LIVING TO WORK

ORANG-UTAN, utterly content in his lush rain forest, sees no pressing need to swing on agile limbs from his soft arboreal bed at dawn. He rises when refreshed, stretching great arms before breakfasting unhurriedly on ripe fruits, and only then carrying on with the business of his day. For Orang-utan understands the true value of time and counsels that you use it wisely. Are you working to live, or living merely to work? Adjust your priorities lest time slips silently away, taking pleasure with it.

ORANG-UTAN
WORKING TO LIVE JOYOUSLY, NOT LIVING TO WORK

CHAMELEON

CONCEAL AMBITION WITH
PATIENCE UNTIL IT IS TIME TO
MAKE YOUR MOVE

CHAMELEON
CONCEAL AMBITION WITH PATIENCE UNTIL IT IS
TIME TO MAKE YOUR MOVE

CHAMELEON is at one with herself and her world, her senses subtle, artful, otherworldly, her very skin sensing her environment and mimicking the colors that surround her. Be aware of subtle energies – the etheric vibrations that emanate from us all, psychic visions from afar – and trust to their message. In the tricky world of business, bide your time. Become gray and unnoticeable, perfectly positioned to assess the myriad currents and independent ambitions at play – and only then, like Chameleon striking a fly, make your move.

RED SQUIRREL
GATHER YOUR RESOURCES NOW, FOR THEY WILL
SUSTAIN YOU THROUGH COMING CHANGE

RED SQUIRREL

GATHER YOUR RESOURCES NOW,
FOR THEY WILL SUSTAIN YOU
THROUGH COMING CHANGE

Benevolent **RED SQUIRREL** has scurried into your cards so that you may prepare for the future, for change is in the air. She counsels that you gather skills that are universal, transferable, and fundamental – the simple tools of life, such as cooking or the growing of vegetables, too often cast aside in a metropolitan world – and preserve some of today's material bounty for the morrow. Unencumbered and adaptable you may then, like Squirrel, swim with the tides of the future and enjoy what is here today.

MOUSE

BE PERSISTENT AND INCISIVE
AND ALL OBSTACLES WILL BE
OVERCOME

MOUSE is tiny and gentle but no shell is so hard that Mouse cannot reach the delicious center within, and no obstacle so tough that it cannot be overcome. As your guide she counsels persistence so you, too, may break through the barriers that block success. Vulnerable to many, Mouse must scrutinize and look beyond the obvious to the pattern within and assess the hidden agenda of others. Emulate Mouse, and your path through life will be safe indeed.

MOUSE
BE PERSISTENT AND INCISIVE AND ALL OBSTACLES
WILL BE OVERCOME

PORCUPINE

YOU MAY DEFEND YOURSELF
HONORABLY WITHOUT HURTING
THOSE CLOSE TO YOU

PORCUPINE trusts in the world. Individual but unterritorial she shares her dens, her favorite verdant pastures, and is rewarded with plenty. But when trust is broken Porcupine defends herself fiercely with barbed quills, causing even Tiger to defer. Like Porcupine, share your bounty with others, be it material or emotional, and discover that it returns to you tenfold. Trust in others while not hesitating in defense and you too will garner the respect that Porcupine commands and the happiness you deserve.

PORCUPINE
YOU MAY DEFEND YOURSELF HONORABLY
WITHOUT HURTING THOSE CLOSE TO YOU

BADGER

ABANDON COMPROMISE AND FIGHT VALIANTLY FOR WHAT YOU BELIEVE IN

BADGER
ABANDON COMPROMISE AND FIGHT VALIANTLY
FOR WHAT YOU BELIEVE IN

Bold **BADGER**, her distinctive stripes a badge of courage, fears none. Throw trepidation and fear aside. Like Badger, abandon compromise and the dissembling that leads to defeat. Take a firm unwavering stand and speak your mind, regardless of others' opinions. Fight valiantly, openly, and aggressively for what you believe in or risk losing it forever. Remember, however, that play is important too. As a cub it honed Badger's awesome skills, as an adult it assures her continued prowess, as it will yours.

SCORPION

IN A NEW RELATIONSHIP PASSION OFFERS THE CHALLENGE OF ECSTASY AND PAIN

SCORPION
IN A NEW RELATIONSHIP PASSION OFFERS THE
CHALLENGE OF ECSTASY AND PAIN

Imbued with powers of such wonder as protecting the mighty Egyptian goddess, Isis, from puissant enemies, **SCORPION** inspires both reverence and respect. Her sting brings forth both death and a potent aphrodisiac for her mate, passion; a reminder that sex affects our psyches in different and powerful ways. At our most vulnerable we can be painfully hurt; at our most passionate, transported into ecstasy. Relationships entered into now will profoundly affect your being. Scorpion counsels that you accept the challenge.

FOX

YOUR SHARPENED SENSES ALLOW YOU TO OBSERVE THE ACTIONS OF OTHERS

FOX
YOUR SHARPENED SENSES ALLOW YOU TO OBSERVE
THE ACTIONS OF OTHERS

Bewitching **Fox**, supreme opportunist, mistress of stealth, observes the world unseen that much may be learned and gained. Fox counsels you hone your senses until they are as sharp as hers and become purposefully conscious and alert to what is happening in the world around you. Soon the interconnectedness of life will become clear, allowing you not only to see the inevitable outcomes to certain situations but, like Fox, to know instinctively when an invitation is an opportunity. Fox counsels that you take it.

TIGER

PASSION AND ADVENTURE BECKON

TIGER
PASSION AND ADVENTURE BECKON

Secure within her own sensuous, controlled power, **TIGER** stalks silently, invisibly, through the magic of the night, securing what her heart desires. Swimming languidly through ancient lakes she conjoins with the water's adaptability, mystical energies, and intuitions. As a messenger, Tiger brings you fresh adventures to change your path, new passions to awaken your heart, and endows you with her powers. Take what she offers and you can transform your life.

HIPPOPOTAMUS

FRIENDS STAND CLOSE BY TO
SHIELD YOU FROM LIFE'S
ADVERSITIES

HIPPOPOTAMUS
FRIENDS STAND CLOSE BY TO SHIELD YOU FROM
LIFE'S ADVERSITIES

Rotund, bountiful **HIPPOPOTAMUS** counsels that you nourish those around you and be nourished in turn. In a world of fast food eaten alone, the time has come to again break bread with friends and family as humankind has always done, and to take succour from confidences given and revealed. These intimates are eyes and ears looking out for us in a complex world and, like the red-lacquered coat of protective liquid that protects Hippopotamus from sunburn and dehydration, they shield us from the vicissitudes of life.

WATER BUFFALO
FACE LIFE HEAD-ON WITH COURAGE AND RECLAIM
THE BRAVE SPIRIT WITHIN YOU

WATER BUFFALO

FACE LIFE HEAD-ON WITH
COURAGE AND RECLAIM THE
BRAVE SPIRIT WITHIN YOU

WATER BUFFALO swims placidly through India's sacred waters, cooling her comfortable rich brown body and languidly wallowing in thick mud. But her pacific, maternal exterior belies a wild, tempestuous nature: she faces life head-on and on great crescent horns tosses enemies determinedly behind her. Tragedy and failure are intrinsic to living but sometimes we are cowed by events, unable to move forward. Mighty Buffalo is the brave spirit within your soul waiting to be reclaimed. Take your courage in both hands and dare to be.

BEAVER
INVESTING IN HOME COMFORTS PROVIDES SECURITY AND FAMILY TOGETHERNESS

BEAVER

INVESTING IN HOME COMFORTS
PROVIDES SECURITY AND FAMILY
TOGETHERNESS

Glossy **BEAVER** counsels conservation in all senses of the word, from protecting the earth's resources for future generations to freeing yourself from large projects that sap your vigor and leave you vulnerable. Beaver mates monogamously for life and keeps her offspring safe until the call of the wild bids them leave. Although our lives may be very different, the archetypal family unit still haunts our dreams. Beaver's lesson is that you turn longing into reality and transform love into a way of life.

ELEPHANT

YOU GAIN THE LOVE AND
WISDOM THAT IS PASSED FROM
ONE GENERATION TO THE NEXT

ELEPHANT
YOU GAIN THE LOVE AND WISDOM THAT IS PASSED
FROM ONE GENERATION TO THE NEXT

A mighty colossus who bestrides the earth on fleshly pillars, **ELEPHANT** is also the embodiment of sentience, heart-felt emotion, altruism, and maternal love. Her intelligent presence in your cards comes to remind you of the unconditional love that only family unreservedly gives us. In times of trouble, in embarrassment we sometimes turn away from even our parents. Elephant counsels that the time has come to accept their love and learn from the wisdom which, like Elephant, they have accrued over a lifetime.

WHALE

THROUGH MUSIC YOU RECLAIM LIFE'S MAGIC AND GROW STRONG IN BODY AND SOUL

WHALE, sublime denizen of the deep oceans, communicates in complex song and serenades his love from afar, telling her of his prowess, experience, and wisdom. We rarely now use our voices except in mundane speech. The cry of triumph, the song of joy, the mystics' chant, and the scream that releases tension all die before they find utterance. Yet rhythm, vibration, and frequency say much and heal both body and soul. Reclaim your voice and, like Whale, grow strong and light as his magic transforms your mind.

WHALE
THROUGH MUSIC YOU RECLAIM LIFE'S MAGIC AND GROW STRONG IN BODY AND SOUL

DOLPHIN

TUNE INTO THE RHYTHM OF YOUR BREATH TO FIND STILLNESS AND PATIENCE

Playful sleek swimmer, gregarious intelligent mammal who sixty million years ago bestrode the earth on four legs, **DOLPHIN** has adapted more elegantly to her world than any other creature. She embodies patience and shows how with time and slow determination you can create wonders, move mountains, and become the person your heart desires. Dolphin must still breathe salty air as she moves rhythmically through the waves and counsels that breathing techniques can heal body and soul, and transport you to other planes.

DOLPHIN
TUNE INTO THE RHYTHM OF YOUR BREATH TO FIND STILLNESS AND PATIENCE

CRAB

SHOW YOUR EMOTIONS AND
REGENERATE LOVE

As **CRAB**'s whole being is synchronized to the waxing and waning of the opalescent Moon so are your body's hormonal and physiological systems tuned to the world's circadian rhythms. Live in harmony with these and your whole being will thrive. Crab is protected by a rigid carapace, but to grow she must risk molting her armor, becoming soft and vulnerable. Like Crab, garner courage and take that risk, be it sporting trial, mental task, or emotional revelation, which offers you regeneration and emotional flowering.

CRAB
SHOW YOUR EMOTIONS AND
REGENERATE LOVE

RAY

COUNTER MALICIOUS TALK BY
CASTING ITS IMPORT FROM
YOUR MIND

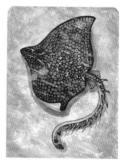

Supreme predator of the blue planet, spiny teeth protrude from **RAY**'s muscular body, delivering a potent toxicant. Teeth help form our words, allowing us to poison others with spite, malice, and lies. If you have been attacked by this fearsome weapon, Ray has come to give you the strength to take heart and cast from your mind the venom that is morphing into ever-more destructive thought. Malice dwelt upon gains strength; ignored, its power diminishes daily.

RAY
COUNTER MALICIOUS TALK BY CASTING ITS
IMPORT FROM YOUR MIND

SEAL

HARD WORK AND INSPIRATION ARE THE FOUNDATION OF TRUE CREATIVITY

SEAL
HARD WORK AND INSPIRATION ARE THE
FOUNDATION OF TRUE CREATIVITY

SEAL inhabits the watery depths from which spring imagination, intuition, the power of dreams, and the infinity of creation. That Seal gives birth on land shows that these landscapes of your mind may be made material. Do your dreams show desires not yet acknowledged? Then the time is ripe to make them your own. True creation and inspiration are also yours, but will remain discarnate without the hard work which alone can give them form. Seal's wisdom is arduous, but its rewards are immense.

OCTOPUS
TRAVEL ACROSS EARTH AND OVER SEA TO
SECURELY EMBRACE YOUR DREAM

OCTOPUS

TRAVEL ACROSS EARTH AND OVER SEA TO SECURELY EMBRACE YOUR DREAM

OCTOPUS does not wait for fate to deliver her dinner of Crab, employing whatever strategy is necessary for his capture, even abandoning water for earth's air. She counsels that you, too, follow your dream. If your partner has left for a faraway land join them; if a new exciting possibility calls from distant climes, embrace it as firmly as Octopus does Crab. If others obstruct you, like Octopus eclipse your actions in an inky cloak until your dream is securely within your grasp.

CROCODILE

THE ALCHEMY OF ENERGY
TEACHES THAT DEATH WILL
ALWAYS YIELD NEW LIFE

Silently slipping through her riverine world, guardian of the margins between land and water, of the mud from which life springs, **CROCODILE** is keeper of all knowledge. Her wisdom speaks both of the enduring nature of life and its utter fragility, of gentleness and ferocity of how death yields life and the constant transformation of all energy. If Crocodile has swum to you, the time has come to examine the primordial mysteries of life and prepare yourself for rebirth and the wonders it will bring.

CROCODILE
THE ALCHEMY OF ENERGY TEACHES THAT DEATH
WILL ALWAYS YIELD NEW LIFE

FROG

ADAPT AND SURVIVE BY
ACCEPTING THE INEVITABLE AND
SEIZING POTENTIAL

Mistress of diversity, **FROG** conforms seamlessly and ingeniously to her environment. If she has leaped into your cards, your strategy must also be to adapt and survive. Sometimes life moves inexorably on and nothing we can do will change events or alter fate. Frog counsels that for now it is wise to accept the inevitable while maximizing even the tiniest of possible advantages. That way you grow strong in the face of adversity and may influence events when opportunity arises.

FROG
ADAPT AND SURVIVE BY ACCEPTING THE
INEVITABLE AND SEIZING POTENTIAL

CHEETAH

A DECISION ONCE MADE WILL BE
FOLLOWED BY UNWAVERING
ACTION

CHEETAH
A DECISION ONCE MADE WILL BE FOLLOWED BY
UNWAVERING ACTION

CHEETAH stalks silently with cat wisdom but pursues her quarry, fleet Gazelle, with the power of sight-hound magic. What other creature partakes of two natures? Look within to discover a plurality of talents and ways of being, for Cheetah is offering you the chance to be exceptional too. If Cheetah, fastest living mammal, has run into your cards, this is not a time for hesitatation: decision followed by unwavering action is now essential. Like Cheetah, grasp what life has to offer.

LION
BANISH LONELINESS BY REACHING OUT TO
SPECIAL FRIENDS

LION

BANISH LONELINESS BY
REACHING OUT TO SPECIAL
FRIENDS

Tawny monarch of the Savannah, **LION** does not waste her days in needless physical exertion, but conserves energy by sleeping, resting, and companionably lounging. Working long, exhausting hours for the money to purchase prestige goods leaves little time for the pleasures of friendship. Loneliness is spirit-diminishing – designer clothes make poor companions. Lion has padded into your cards to remind you how vital friends and neighbors really are. Reach out to those around you and be open to others.

COBRA

CHANGE IS INEVITABLE, BUT
WITH IT COMES THE CHANCE TO
SHED A BURDEN

Incomparable, charismatic snake, guardian of water and savior of grain, **COBRA** counsels you consider your fundamental needs, feeding your body with energized whole foods and walking amongst nature, for change and rebirth are now inevitable and require your vitality. Fear not for the future, for as Cobra sloughs her old skin so will you shed that which holds you back. Look carefully at the meaning of desire before letting its deep sexual energy free, for as Cobra knows only that which is given in mutual love can transform.

COBRA
CHANGE IS INEVITABLE, BUT WITH IT COMES THE
CHANCE TO SHED A BURDEN

KANGAROO

AS EVENTS TAKE ON THEIR OWN
MOMENTUM YOU TAKE A TRUE
LEAP FORWARD

KANGAROO burns energy quickly when first she begins to hop, but once her rhythm is set she bounds tirelessly under a warm sun. It is time to banish obstacles, be they fears which lurk in the dark hidden recesses of your mind or more tangible problems. They may seem insurmountable, but Kangaroo knows that after you take that first leap forward events will take on their own momentum and you, like Kangaroo, who cannot move backward, will have no option but to go forward, your burdens falling behind you.

KANGAROO
AS EVENTS TAKE ON THEIR OWN MOMENTUM YOU
TAKE A TRUE LEAP FORWARD

HARE

DISCERNMENT BEFORE A PASSIONATE ENCOUNTER LEADS TO THE MAGIC OF LOVE

HARE
DISCERNMENT BEFORE A PASSIONATE ENCOUNTER
LEADS TO THE MAGIC OF LOVE

HARE travels lightly, unfettered, and counsels that you, too, jettison worries that tether you to the present and tie you to the past, cleansing and lightening your mind through meditation or by sharing your fears with another. Unburdened, you may then react quickly as the future speedily unfolds, avoiding disaster and seizing opportunity. Hare knows how fragile is the heart. If deeply drawn to another, look first into their mind and soul. For it is discernment followed by passion that leads to the magic of love.

WOLF
LISTEN TO YOUR INNER WISDOM AND ENJOY THE
GIFT OF FREEDOM

WOLF

LISTEN TO YOUR INNER WISDOM AND ENJOY THE GIFT OF FREEDOM

Wild, intelligent spirit of the plains and forests, **WOLF** takes what he needs, no more, no less, and counsels you to do the same. He instinctively trusts in his acute physical senses and the strong co-operative bonds of his complex social group, and is rewarded with freedom. Follow his confident, firm paw prints down uncharted tracks, listen attentively to your own inner voice as you walk, trusting in the strength of the relationships you value and the gift of brother Wolf, which sets you free.

RHINOCEROS

STILL THE CHATTER WITHIN
TO SEE YOUR TRUE PATH
IN LIFE

RHINOCEROS
STILL THE CHATTER WITHIN TO SEE YOUR TRUE
PATH IN LIFE

Ancient behemoth, repository of primordial wisdoms, **RHINO**, like supreme masters has no need for society. Rhino stands sturdily in your cards to counsel that you still the constant chatter in your head, take time out from hectic socializing, and simply be. At first your mind will echo with a thousand thoughts, but soon it will quieten and the true nature of your path and dreams will make themselves known. And with Rhino by your side, you may turn them into reality.

MOUNTAIN GOAT

FIGHTING FOR LOVE OR ARDENT
DECLARATIONS MAY HIDE
UNFAITHFULNESS

MOUNTAIN GOAT
FIGHTING FOR LOVE OR ARDENT DECLARATIONS
MAY HIDE UNFAITHFULNESS

Deep in his body, mystical **GOAT** fashions beozar, considered a remedy for disease. As Goat holds these cures within, so you hold the remedies for your life's ills. Goat, intensely sexual, maintains a harem and fights fiercely for his consorts and counsels that even those who strive ardently for your love may not be true. However, defend your present love passionately and thoughtfully, celebrate it with the gift of wild rose, the full Moon seen on a wild night, and it will remain yours forever.

LLAMA

LET COURAGE LEAD YOU TO SEEK
SUPPORT AND OVERCOME A FEAR
OF INTIMACY

LLAMA
LET COURAGE LEAD YOU TO SEEK SUPPORT AND
OVERCOME A FEAR OF INTIMACY

Sweet-tempered, soft, and friendly, **LLAMA**'s gentle and beautiful wide-eyed face belies her ability to withstand unforgiving conditions. Llama counsels that defensiveness keeps others far away while drawing near loneliness and disrespect. Let go of angst and foreboding, perhaps by consulting another who may untangle the psychology of your mind. As no path is impassable to Llama, with courage you may take a hard but rewarding road to rediscover the sweetness in your soul and be as one with others.

WILD BOAR
WHATEVER TRADITION OR OTHERS EXPECT OF
YOU, ONLY TO YOURSELF BE TRUE

WILD BOAR

WHATEVER TRADITION OR
OTHERS EXPECT OF YOU, ONLY
TO YOURSELF BE TRUE

Jungle lore casts meaty **WILD BOAR** as a banquet for others, but Boar reverses the role of predator and prey proving tradition wrong. If you allow society or individuals to dictate the part you play in life, constant friction between outer persona and inner desire will cause stress, deep unhappiness and, with time, coruscating resentment. If your role is a sham then your relationships with others will also be false. Boar counsels that you be true to yourself so that you may in turn be true to others.

WILD HORSE

SPEAK YOUR PASSION ALOUD
AND DEFEND THOSE WHOM YOU
LOVE IN WORD AND DEED

WILD HORSE
SPEAK YOUR PASSION ALOUD AND DEFEND THOSE
WHOM YOU LOVE IN WORD AND DEED

WILD HORSE, fabulous winged-Pegasus returned to earth, is the epitome of male sexual energy and of the soaring spirit which dance sets free. His passions and intentions toward his mares are openly declared, his defence of them vigorous. Strong at heart, Horse knows no fear of others or of rejection. Like Horse, defend robustly those whom you love from those who would hurt or belittle them, and let them know of your feelings with ardent speech – for Horse knows that Cupid favors the brave.

SCARAB BEETLE

WHAT IS UNREGARDED OR
DISCARDED HOLDS A SECRET,
A SEED OF CREATION

SCARAB BEETLE
WHAT IS UNREGARDED OR DISCARDED HOLDS
A SECRET, A SEED OF CREATION

Armored shining jewel, Egypt's sacred symbol, **SCARAB** generates life from the waste of others. Look at what you discard or even despise, for within its form lie the germs of creation. For some this may mean procreation; for others, artistic creation as symbolized by the flowering of the seeds buried in Scarab's ball of dung. Consider also those unregarded in the river of your life. One may be the catalyst for a new endeavor, another hold unguessed-at knowledge, or even the secret that will unlock your heart.

BEAR

NURTURE CREATIVITY AND
RETURN TO THE SWEETNESS
OF LIFE

BEAR
NURTURE CREATIVITY AND RETURN TO THE
SWEETNESS OF LIFE

BEAR prepares for the birth of her cubs by building up reserves of nourishing fat, but unless conditions are perfect she will not give birth to her fleshly creations – for Bear knows that timing and preparation are all. Deliberate carefully before bringing anything into being and nurture your creativity by withdrawal, whether in meditation or retreat. When you return to the material world your ideas will bear fleshy ripe fruits, and you will again discover the sweetness that life offers you.

DEER
TAKE NOTE OF THE MESSAGES IN WHISPERS AND
SECRETS ADRIFT ON THE BREEZE

DEER

TAKE NOTE OF THE MESSAGES IN
WHISPERS AND SECRETS ADRIFT
ON THE BREEZE

Hind, gentle, alert, every sense keen, stands motionless amongst the leafy trees. Like **DEER**, be acutely aware now of what drifts to you on the breeze. A snippet of conversation, even the fresh spice of cologne, may hold secrets untold. Deer protects herself by gathering peacefully with others and counsels that you now seek to be part of a bigger whole. If estranged from family or friends, Deer advises that the sagacious ask for forgiveness and forgive in turn, fostering mutual love and the regeneration that this brings.

BISON
RECOGNIZE THE RICHES OF THE PAST AND THE ABUNDANCE OF THE PRESENT

Monolithic **BISON**, ancient, magnificent wild lord of the grassland prairies, embodies strength and endurance. Unchanging Bison has flourished where other mammals have become extinct and counsels that you too draw upon the riches of the past. Look into your family tree to discover your unique cultural heritage. Transmute the old and seemingly worthless to a vibrant new form, or study to rediscover fabulous lost processes or wisdom. The time for abundance is coming, but you must be prepared to recognize its gifts.

BISON
RECOGNIZE THE RICHES OF THE PAST AND THE ABUNDANCE OF THE PRESENT

MOOSE
WITH SELF-RELIANCE AND MEASURED PATIENCE ADVERSITY WILL BE OVERCOME

Mythic **MOOSE**, primal in her power, ranges mysteriously alone through the world's great boreal forests, taking her own decisions and vigorously defending herself with sharp hooves and mighty charges. Moose teaches the self-reliance that develops strength of character and the ability to overcome adversity. Secure, Moose has no need to rush into love and

MOOSE
WITH SELF-RELIANCE AND MEASURED PATIENCE ADVERSITY WILL BE OVERCOME

thereby court failure. She counsels that you, too, let love come in its own time and so create a relationship of trust, profundity, and true meaning.

BABOON

IN LOVE AND DECLARATIONS OF
PASSION HEARTFELT
COMMUNICATION IS THE KEY

BABOON
IN LOVE AND DECLARATIONS OF PASSION
HEARTFELT COMMUNICATION IS THE KEY

Sublime **BABOON**, adept of love, wears her heart on her sleeve. Baboon does not pretend. Her passions and shows of affection are genuine, her reactions without artifice, so you may believe the ardent declarations of others. Truthful, heartfelt communication and open expression of feelings are what matter now in your relationship if, like Baboon, you seek lasting love. Hiding your emotions will leave others unsure of your intentions and reluctant to reveal their feelings, which can only lead to misunderstandings and sadness.

TORTOISE
WHEN CHANGES ARE MADE FOR THE SAKE OF
CHANGE ITSELF, RESIST

TORTOISE

WHEN CHANGES ARE MADE FOR
THE SAKE OF CHANGE ITSELF,
RESIST

Older than Dinosaur, embodiment of ancient wisdom and living testament to the wonder of her form, unchanging **TORTOISE** plods on through time. Like Tortoise, resist change for novelty's sake. Be true to your way of living, your partner, and your creativity, lest you destroy something more wonderful than you yet know. Tortoise also counsels constructing a mental carapace to protect yourself from the unjustified criticisms of others, for as Tortoise's hatchlings emerge from their shells, perfect, you too were born flawless.

ACKNOWLEDGMENTS

I would like to thank my publisher, Cindy Richards, for her patience and vision; my editor, Liz Dean, for her sensitivity and understanding; Csaba Pasztor for the beauty of his illustrations, which show so clearly the souls of the animals within; Nick Ilott for his kindly help, and all the rest of the team at Cico Books.

I would also like to thank my friend Nicola for providing me with the Indian sanctuary where I wrote the majority of this book, and Margaret, who nurtured so well my dear dog, Poppy, in my absence.

EAGLE
CREATE YOUR VISION

OWL
SEEK OUT DEEPER KNOWLEDGE TO SEE THROUGH DECEPTION

HUMMING BIRD
TURN AWAY FROM INFIDELITY SO THAT
LOVE MAY BLOSSOM

PARROT
LET SUNSHINE REVITALIZE YOUR SOUL AND COLOR
TRANSFORM YOUR WORLD

PEACOCK
PROTECT YOUR HEART FROM THOSE WHO MAY
CHEAT BEFORE THEY HURT YOU

BUTTERFLY
DELIGHT IN LIFE AND EMBRACE CHANGE AS THE
SOURCE OF YOUR CREATIVITY

BAT
You have the power to transcend failure and move into a limitless future

SPIDER
**TRAVEL WILL OPEN UP NEW POSSIBILITIES
AND ONE SPECIAL CONNECTION**

BEE
HARD WORK IS REWARDED WITH RESPONSIBILITY
AND A SWEETNESS THAT IS SHARED

BLACK PANTHER
SENSUALITY AND PASSION STIR BENEATH A
CLOAK OF SECRECY

PANDA
ENJOY THE SANCTUARY OF SOLITUDE TO REGAIN SELF-ESTEEM AND TRANQUILITY

SLOTH
CONSIDER THE SMALLNESS OF YOUR NEEDS AND
TREASURE WHAT YOU POSSESS

ORANG-UTAN
WORKING TO LIVE JOYOUSLY, NOT LIVING
TO WORK

RED SQUIRREL
GATHER YOUR RESOURCES NOW, FOR THEY WILL
SUSTAIN YOU THROUGH COMING CHANGE

MOUSE
BE PERSISTENT AND INCISIVE AND ALL OBSTACLES WILL BE OVERCOME

PORCUPINE
Y\ou may defend yourself honorably
without hurting those close to you

BADGER
ABANDON COMPROMISE AND FIGHT VALIANTLY
FOR WHAT YOU BELIEVE IN

SCORPION
IN A NEW RELATIONSHIP PASSION OFFERS THE
CHALLENGE OF ECSTASY AND PAIN

FOX
YOUR SHARPENED SENSES ALLOW YOU TO OBSERVE THE ACTIONS OF OTHERS

TIGER
PASSION AND ADVENTURE BECKON

HIPPOPOTAMUS
FRIENDS STAND CLOSE BY TO SHIELD YOU FROM
LIFE'S ADVERSITIES

WATER BUFFALO
FACE LIFE HEAD-ON WITH COURAGE AND RECLAIM
THE BRAVE SPIRIT WITHIN YOU

BEAVER
Investing in home comforts provides
security and family togetherness

ELEPHANT
YOU GAIN THE LOVE AND WISDOM THAT IS PASSED
FROM ONE GENERATION TO THE NEXT

WHALE
THROUGH MUSIC YOU RECLAIM LIFE'S MAGIC AND
GROW STRONG IN BODY AND SOUL

DOLPHIN
TUNE INTO THE RHYTHM OF YOUR BREATH TO
FIND STILLNESS AND PATIENCE

CRAB
SHOW YOUR EMOTIONS AND
REGENERATE LOVE

RAY
**COUNTER MALICIOUS TALK BY CASTING ITS
IMPORT FROM YOUR MIND**

SEAL
**HARD WORK AND INSPIRATION ARE THE
FOUNDATION OF TRUE CREATIVITY**

OCTOPUS
TRAVEL ACROSS EARTH AND OVER SEA TO
SECURELY EMBRACE YOUR DREAM

CROCODILE
THE ALCHEMY OF ENERGY TEACHES THAT DEATH
WILL ALWAYS YIELD NEW LIFE

FROG
ADAPT AND SURVIVE BY ACCEPTING THE
INEVITABLE AND SEIZING POTENTIAL

CHEETAH
A DECISION ONCE MADE WILL BE FOLLOWED BY UNWAVERING ACTION

LION
**BANISH LONELINESS BY REACHING OUT TO
SPECIAL FRIENDS**

COBRA
CHANGE IS INEVITABLE, BUT WITH IT COMES THE CHANCE TO SHED A BURDEN

KANGAROO
AS EVENTS TAKE ON THEIR OWN MOMENTUM YOU
TAKE A TRUE LEAP FORWARD

HARE
DISCERNMENT BEFORE A PASSIONATE ENCOUNTER
LEADS TO THE MAGIC OF LOVE

WOLF
LISTEN TO YOUR INNER WISDOM AND ENJOY THE
GIFT OF FREEDOM

RHINOCEROS
STILL THE CHATTER WITHIN TO SEE YOUR TRUE
PATH IN LIFE

MOUNTAIN GOAT
FIGHTING FOR LOVE OR ARDENT DECLARATIONS
MAY HIDE UNFAITHFULNESS

LLAMA
LET COURAGE LEAD YOU TO SEEK SUPPORT AND OVERCOME A FEAR OF INTIMACY

WILD BOAR
WHATEVER TRADITION OR OTHERS EXPECT OF
YOU, ONLY TO YOURSELF BE TRUE

WILD HORSE
SPEAK YOUR PASSION ALOUD AND DEFEND THOSE
WHOM YOU LOVE IN WORD AND DEED

SCARAB BEETLE
WHAT IS UNREGARDED OR DISCARDED HOLDS
A SECRET, A SEED OF CREATION

BEAR
NURTURE CREATIVITY AND RETURN TO THE
SWEETNESS OF LIFE

DEER
TAKE NOTE OF THE MESSAGES IN WHISPERS AND
SECRETS ADRIFT ON THE BREEZE

BISON
RECOGNIZE THE RICHES OF THE PAST AND THE ABUNDANCE OF THE PRESENT

MOOSE
WITH SELF-RELIANCE AND MEASURED PATIENCE
ADVERSITY WILL BE OVERCOME

BABOON
IN LOVE AND DECLARATIONS OF PASSION
HEARTFELT COMMUNICATION IS THE KEY

TORTOISE
**WHEN CHANGES ARE MADE FOR THE SAKE OF
CHANGE ITSELF, RESIST**